Date: 4/3/14

BR 636.107 KUS
Kuskowski, Alex.
Foals /

Foals

Alex Kuskowski

A Division of ABDO

ABDO
Publishing Company

Consulting Editor, Diane Craig, M.A./Reading Specialist

visit us at www.abdopublishing.com

Published by ABDO Publishing Company, a division of ABDO, P.O. Box 398166, Minneapolis, Minnesota 55439. Copyright © 2014 by Abdo Consulting Group, Inc. International copyrights reserved in all countries. No part of this book may be reproduced in any form without written permission from the publisher. SandCastle™ is a trademark and logo of ABDO Publishing Company.

Printed in the United States of America, North Mankato, Minnesota
062013
092013

 PRINTED ON RECYCLED PAPER

Editor: Liz Salzmann
Content Developer: Alex Kuskowski
Cover and Interior Design and Production: Mighty Media, Inc.
Photo Credits: Shutterstock, Thinkstock

Library of Congress Cataloging-in-Publication Data

Kuskowski, Alex.
  Foals / by Alex Kuskowski ; consulting editor, Diane Craig, M.A./Reading Specialist.
    pages cm. -- (Baby animals)
  Audience: 4-9.
  ISBN 978-1-61783-837-8
  1. Foals--Juvenile literature. I. Title.
  SF309.2.K87 2014
  636.1'6--dc23
                          2012049662

SandCastle™ Level: Beginning

SandCastle™ books are created by a team of professional educators, reading specialists, and content developers around five essential components—phonemic awareness, phonics, vocabulary, text comprehension, and fluency—to assist young readers as they develop reading skills and strategies and increase their general knowledge. All books are written, reviewed, and leveled for guided reading, early reading intervention, and Accelerated Reader® programs for use in shared, guided, and independent reading and writing activities to support a balanced approach to literacy instruction. The SandCastle™ series has four levels that correspond to early literacy development. The levels are provided to help teachers and parents select appropriate books for young readers.

Emerging Readers
(no flags)

Beginning Readers
(1 flag)

Transitional Readers
(2 flags)

Fluent Readers
(3 flags)

Contents

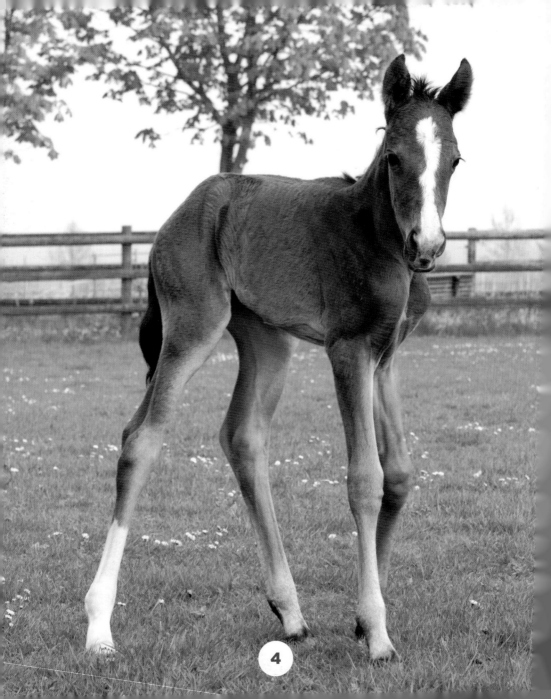

4

Foals

A baby horse is a foal.
Foals live on farms.

Foals can sleep standing up or lying down. Foals sleep in **stables** at night.

A foal stays close to its mother. It feels safe in a herd.

Foals are thin and tall.
They have long legs.

Dusty is Elliot's foal.
Elliot pets Dusty on
the nose.

Ava's foal bends down to eat. Foals eat grass and grains. They also drink their mothers' milk.

Foals have a lot of **energy**. They like to **gallop**.

Foals are social animals.
They play together.

Julia walks with her foal. Foals need exercise to stay healthy.

Did You Know?

▶ A foal can stand and walk less than an hour after being born.

▶ A foal's **height** is measured in hands. A hand equals 4 inches (10 cm).

▶ Foals are fully grown horses at four to five years old.

▶ Horses have the largest eyes of any land **mammal**.

Foal Quiz

Read each sentence below. Then decide whether it is true or false.

1. Foals sleep in **stables** at night.

2. Elliot pets Dusty on her neck.

3. Foals only eat grass.

4. Foals like to **gallop**.

5. Foals do not need exercise.

Answers: 1. True 2. False 3. False 4. True 5. False

Glossary

energy – the ability to move, work, or play hard without getting tired.

gallop – to run fast so that all four feet are off the ground at the same time once in each stride.

height – how tall something is.

mammal – a warm-blooded animal that has hair and whose females produce milk to feed their young.

stable – a building, such as a barn, where animals live and eat.